To our loving parents, Dolores and Eugene Wiegand and Lorraine and John Hoffman, for all of the sacrifices that they made and the love that they provided so that we could share in a memorable college experience.

- Polly and John

About the Authors

Polly and John Hoffman are both graduates of the University of Notre Dame, where they met as students. They also received their master's degrees from Indiana University. Their inspiration for this book was the significant sacrifices that their parents made so that they could have the opportunity to be a part of the Notre Dame experience. Recognizing the sacrifices that all parents make in supporting college education, they wanted to do a series of books customized to the individual university experiences and the opportunities they offer. In developing the series, they had the opportunity to learn about the unique traditions, memories, and experiences of several universities. While there is no way to ever adequately express their gratitude, the book will hopefully provide students and alumni with an opportunity to say "thank you" to those that supported them in a special personalized and memorable manner.

www.mascotbooks.com

Cover photo by Virginia Tech, Schuminweb via Flickr, Hector Alejandro via Flickr, Erich Geist via Flickr, Barb Lipes via Flickr, Carrie E. Cox via Flickr, Tech Sports via Flickr, US Fish & Wildlife via Flickr, Chuck Mummert via Flickr, Danial Lin via Flickr, Giving to Virginia Tech via Flickr, Ray Homoroc via Flickr, Virginia Tech, Sherry Ezhuthachan via Flickr, B Wendell jones via Flickr, Wikipedia, Virginia Tech Jim Stroup, Techsports via Flickr, Giving to Virginia Tech via Flickr, Gary Cope, Class of 1997, Steven M. via Flickr, Craig Eddy via Flickr, Goheels.com, Katie (AlaskaHokie) via Flickr, Virginia Tech, Roger Gupta, Virginia Tech, Sherry Ezhuthachan via Flickr, Virginia Tech, Techsports via Flickr, Balfour.com, Virginia Tech, US Department of Agriculture via Flickr, Christopher Bowns via Flickr, Wikipedia, Bret Salmons via Flickr, Thetejon via Flickr, Chuck Mummert via Flickr, Gerry Brague via Flickr, Tracie Gardner via Flickr, Virginia Tech

For more information, please contact:
Mascot Books
560 Herndon Parkway #120
Herndon, VA 20170
info@mascotbooks.com

CPSIA Code: PRT0914A
ISBN-13: 978-1-62086-879-9

Printed in the United States

Thank You for

VIRGINIA TECH™

John & Polly Hoffman

Dear _____ ,

There is no way that I could ever adequately express my gratitude for the support you provided so that I could experience Virginia Tech in its full glory.

But I would like to say,

_____

_____

_____

_____

_____

_____

Thank You for

VIRGINIA TECH™

Thank you for...

...that breathtaking first view of Burruss Hall.

FACT

Burruss Hall is named for eighth president Julian Ashby Burruss. In the 1920s, he admitted women as full-time students and cut the four-year military requirement for male students to two years, setting the stage for a larger civilian student body. He also organized a chapter of Phi Kappa Phi, put off-campus living to the test, brought athletics under the supervision of college authorities, and established the Engineering Experiment Station and Engineering Extension Division. Burruss was president from 1919 to 1945.

http://www.vt.edu/about/buildings/burruss-hall.html

...giving me the confidence to go full speed ahead into freshman orientation.

FACT

Admissions directors use a holistic approach throughout the application review process. Many factors are considered, the most important being rigor of academic program, grades in academic courses, and standardized test scores.

http://www.admiss.vt.edu/apply/what-we-look-for/

...the exhilaration of hearing The Marching Virginians take the field for the first time.

...the thunderous burst of Skipper cannon.

FACT

On the way back to show the new cannon to the whole Corps, its originators learned that President John F. Kennedy had been shot and killed.

They wanted to do something in honor of our fallen Head of State. They remembered an old military tradition that, at the death of a President, all military installations give a 50 gun salute to their fallen leader. It was then that they knew what they had to name the new cannon. It would be named "Skipper" in honor of John Fitzgerald Kennedy and his naval background.

http://spec.lib.vt.edu/archives/125th/cadets/cannon.htm

...the delight of biting into a famous Lane Stadium turkey leg.

...the passionate outcries of my fellow students cheering the Hokies at Cassell Coliseum.

FACT

Built as a replacement for the much smaller War Memorial Gymnasium, the Coliseum's construction began in 1961. It was fully completed in December 1964. The first game was on January 3, 1962 when the Hokies played Alabama. The Hokies won 91-67. Unfortunately, the crowd sat on the concrete floor to watch the game because the seats had not arrived.

http://en.wikipedia.org/wiki/Cassell_Coliseum

...the sense of fulfillment from providing service to others as part of The Big Event.

...the majestic countenance of buildings made from Hokie Stone.

FACT

Virginia Tech was born as a land-grant college and, appropriately, its distinctive buildings have been constructed from the product of Southwest Virginia geology. The university mines the distinguishing limestone at its own quarry on the fringes of Blacksburg. Originally called "our native stone," the rock has become known more familiarly, and more affectionately, as Hokie Stone.

http://www.vt.edu/about/traditions/hokie-stone.html

...the bonding that occurs between students and alumni when we proudly wear the Maroon and Orange.

FACT

The first school colors, black and cadet gray, were picked in 1891 by the new student-run Athletic Association to reflect the principal colors of the cadet uniforms worn by the all-male, military student body. But when the black and gray appeared on athletic uniforms in the striped style popular in the late 19th century, athletes complained that the stripes made them look like convicts.

The corps of cadets and a few other people from the college then banded together to examine the question of colors. They discovered that no other college or university in the country had orange and maroon as its school colors, so burnt orange and Chicago maroon were adopted in 1896 as the official colors.

https://www.unirel.vt.edu/history/students_alumni/traditions.html

...the architectural elegance of Torgersen Hall.

FACT

Called the Advanced Communications and Information Technology Center in the building proposal and during construction, Torgersen includes 30-miles of fiber-optic cable and 75-miles of copper cable. It houses offices, laboratory space, classrooms, space for televised distance learning, and two auditoriums. The first floor includes an atrium with computer hookups that serves as an electronic study court. The building joins Newman Library via an enclosed bridge that spans Alumni Mall and provides reading-room space.

https://www.vt.edu/about/buildings/torgersen-hall.html

...those picnics at the duck pond.

FACT

Construction started in 1934 with funds supplied by Civil Works Administration ($18,821 for three projects). Named "Duck Pond" by students. Fed by Stroubles Creek and a smaller lake, Ice Pond, slightly above and to north. The two ponds serve as year-round homes principally to flocks of Canadian geese and mallard ducks.

http://www.unirel.vt.edu/history/physical_plant/miscellaneous_campus_features.html

...the ability to explain exactly what a "Hokie" is.

...Tuesday night karaoke and Rails at TOTS.

FACT

Top of the Stairs (popularly known as TOTS) is a bar and restaurant in Blacksburg, Virginia, near the Virginia Tech campus. Established in 1978, TOTS is popular among Virginia Tech students and alumni due to its history, proximity to campus, signature mixed drink known as the Rail, and Tuesday night karaoke.

http://www.topofthestairs.com/

...the excitement of watching Hokie baseball.

...the wit and wisdom that only the *Collegiate Times* could provide.

...the wonderful memories of the Ring Dance.

FACT

A tradition dating from 1934, the Virginia Tech Ring Dance symbolizes a hallmark in a Tech student's career. Upon entering the dance, each couple receives a pair of ribbons in the class colors. The lady wears her date's ring on her wrist with the darker colored ribbon, and the gentleman wears his date's ring on his wrist with the lighter colored ribbon. At the official Ring Exchange, the Corps of Cadets enter the ballroom and stand in the shape of the Class numerals. As each couple exchanges rings, "Moonlight and VPI," written specifically for the Ring Dance by composer Fred Waring and lyricist Charles Gaynor, is sung. As the clock strikes midnight, the evening ends with an elaborate fireworks display on the Drillfield, and the playing of "Silvertaps."

http://www.alumni.vt.edu/traditions/

...the sense of pride and patriotism when watching the Corps of Cadets.

FACT The Virginia Tech Corps of Cadets (VTCC) is the military component of the student body at Virginia Polytechnic Institute and State University. Cadets live together in dormitories, march to meals in formation, wear a distinctive uniform on campus, and receive an intensive military and leadership educational experience similar to that available at the United States service academies. The Corps of Cadets has existed from the founding of the Virginia Agricultural and Mechanical College in 1872 to the present-day institution of Virginia Tech, which is designated a senior military college by federal law.

http://en.wikipedia.org/wiki/Virginia_Tech_Corps_of_Cadets

...the majesty and symbolism of the Pylons.

FACT

The War Memorial Chapel contains eight pylons. The upper level contains Memorial Court with eight sculptured Indiana limestone pylons representing from left to right: Brotherhood, Honor, Leadership, Sacrifice, Service, Loyalty, Duty, and Ut Prosim (the University motto, "That I May Serve").

https://www.vt.edu/about/buildings/war-memorial-chapel.html

...the sense of spirit when chanting the Old Hokie Yell.

WORSHAM FIELD

SunTrust

AEP APPALACHIAN POWER

VT

...the rush of adrenaline when the team enters to "Enter Sandman."

...the sense of pride when listening to the band play "Tech Triumph."

FACT

Wilfred Preston (Pete) Maddux, a trombone and baritone player in the Virginia Tech Regimental Band (member from the Fall of 1917 to 1919), jointly composed "Tech Triumph" in 1919 along with Mattie Walton Eppes (Boggs). Mattie Eppes was a neighbor of Pete in his hometown of Blackstone, Virginia. When he was home, Pete would often play violin with Mattie accompanying him on the piano. One evening in the summer of 1919, Pete asked her to help him compose a fight song for VPI. She played the tune and Pete wrote out the score and the words for two verses in a single evening.

http://en.wikipedia.org/wiki/Tech_Triumph

...the tenacity of the competitive spirit of the Hokie women's soccer team.

FACT

The Virginia Tech Hokies women's soccer team began in 1980 with two club teams under the guidance of Everett Germain and his two daughter's Betsy and Julie. Women's soccer has made great strides over the years and continues to be very successful.

http://en.wikipedia.org/wiki/Virginia_Tech_Hokies_women's_soccer

...the challenge of getting my picture taken with ALL of the painted HokieBirds.

...the patriotic pride from watching the "Highty Tighties".

FACT

By 1919, the Regimental Band began to be known as the Highty-Tighties . Just like "Hokie" began as part of a cadet cheer, so too, the name "Highty-Tighty" began as part of a cadet cheer.

http://www.band.vtcc.vt.edu/history.php

...the sense of community when we all join in the Hokie Pokie.

...the bonding that develops when participating in the Cadet vs. Civilian Snowball Fight.

FACT

Virginia Tech began as a Reserve Officer Training Corp school. Today the university takes all comers, but the ROTC heritage lives on in the annual Cadet vs. Civilian Snowball Fight. A fire alarm sounds during the first big snowfall of the year—a signal for the student body to launch an all-campus snowball fight on the Drill Field. The annual battle has the look of medieval combat, snowball style.

http://mom.me/mind-body/4337-weirdest-college-rituals/item/22782-2-virginia-tech/

...the majestic beauty of the Cascades.

FACT

Technically a national recreation area rather than a national park, the Cascades offer many amenities to its visitors. It is a popular destination of Virgina Tech students. The Cascades are fed by Mountain Lake which is the highest natural lake in Virginia and consistently records the lowest temperatures in the whole state.

http://www.collegiatetimes.com/lifestyle/article_d72444da-bdf7-52eb-aa95-f46e394ae2f4.html?mode=jqm

...the thrill of that first touchdown celebration.

FACT

Virginia Agricultural and Mechanical College first played football on October 21, 1892 against St. Albans Lutheran Boys School (Radford, Virginia). The game took place on a plowed off wheat field that was "about as level as a side of Brush Mountain." The Hokies won their first game 14-10, but were defeated 10-0 eight days later on a return trip to Radford.

http://en.wikipedia.org/wiki/Virginia_Tech_Hokies_football

...the excitement of the annual unveiling of the class ring.

...the delicious campus cuisine.

FACT

Dining Services boasts a tradition of award-winning programming, venues, and service. In the last five years, more than 50 colleges and businesses have benchmarked the program and its facilities. It has received numerous awards for its chefs, facilities, franchises, and program, including:
2014 RecycleMania Pledge Drive Winner
No. 3 Best College for Food in America - Daily Meal
No. 1 Top Universities for Food & Dining - Ranked by Students - Cappex College Insider
http://www.dining.vt.edu/about/awards.html

...the unique opportunity to be around so many extraordinary people.

FACT

On average, about 41% of each freshmen class graduated in the top 10% of their high schools, and 83% graduated in the top 25%.

http://www.vt.edu/about/factbook/student-overview.html

...the
beauty of
the sunsets
on campus.

...the fun of watching the HokieBird bench press after each score.

FACT

After scoring in football, the VT cheerleaders carry out a bench and weights for the HokieBird to perform bench presses. He does one press for every point VT has scored. Sometimes, in lieu of bench presses, the HokieBird has done sit-ups or push-ups.

http://en.wikipedia.org/wiki/HokieBird

...the competitive juices that flowed when playing rec sports.

FACT

The Department of Recreational Sports enhances the quality of life for the university community by educating and encouraging participation in activities that promote healthy lifestyles, social interactions, and leadership skills. Over 24,000 undergraduate students currently participate.

https://gobblerconnect.vt.edu/organization/www_recsports_vt_edu/about

...the value that a top-tier education will bring me for the rest of my life.

...the knowledge that whatever I do, I should always "reach for excellence."

...the pride that I feel for being a part of one of the greatest alumni networks in the world.

...the wonderful legacy of being a Hokie for the rest of my life.

...for supporting me so that I could pursue my dreams.

FACT

Virginia Tech has a geographically diverse student body.

Top five home states of out-of-state freshmen:
1. Maryland 2. New Jersey 3. Pennsylvania 4. North Carolina 5. New York

Number of states and territories represented (including the District of Columbia): 43
Countries represented: 43
http://www.vt.edu/about/factbook/student-overview.html